The Funny Songbook

BY

ESTHER L. NELSON

ILLUSTRATIONS BY JOYCE BEHR

Sterling Publishing Co. Inc. New York
Distributed in the U.K. by Blandford Press

Other Books of Interest

Best Singing Games for Children of All Ages
Dancing Games for Children of All Ages
Holiday Singing and Dancing Games
Movement Games for Children of All Ages
Musical Games for Children of All Ages
Silly Songbook
Singing and Dancing Games for the Very Young

Thanks to my friends—young, middle-aged and old—who have contributed to this collection of songs: Karen Levine, Lillian Enfield, Barbara Fisher, Susan Braiding, Sheila Gladstone, Noah Feinstein, Walter Moxon, Fay Storch, Joy Yelin, Gerry Hill, Ruth Jacobson, Deb Mapes, Anne Kallem, Estelle Katz, Hannah Reich, Dr. Margot Tallmer, Joyce Kingsboro, Karen Peterson.

To my daughter, Risa Sokolsky, who ferreted out songs from many corners, an added thanks.

And thanks, too, to my dear friend and editor Sheila Barry, whose keen mind, gentle, firm demands and total expertise make the hard work a joyful task.

Library of Congress Cataloging in Publication Data
Main entry under title:

The funny songbook.

For voice and piano ; with chord symbols for guitar.
Summary: An illustrated collection of sixty, easy-to-play, humorous songs including camp songs, parodies, Bible songs, and silly ditties.
1. Children's songs. 2. Humorous songs. [1. Songs. 2. Humorous songs] I. Nelson, Esther L. II. Behr, Joyce, ill.
M1997.F996 1984 84-89
ISBN 0-8069-4682-2
ISBN 0-8069-7832-5 (pbk.)
ISBN 0-8069-4683-0 (lib. bdg.)

Third Printing, 1984

Published by Sterling Publishing Co., Inc.
Two Park Avenue, New York, N.Y. 10016
Distributed in Australia by Oak Tree Press Co., Ltd.
P.O. Box K514 Haymarket, Sydney 2000, N.S.W.
Distributed in the United Kingdom by Blandford Press
Link House, West Street, Poole, Dorset BH15 1LL, England
Distributed in Canada by Oak Tree Press Ltd.
% Canadian Manda Group, P.O. Box 920, Station U
Toronto, Ontario M8Z 5P9
Manufactured in the United States of America

CONTENTS

To the memory of Becky Perces . . .
a rare and beautiful person . . .
and such a lovely dancer . . . with love

GOING BUGGY

The Ants Go Marching

To the tune of "When Johnny Comes Marching Home"

The Ants Go Marching

The ants go marching one by one, hur-
rah, hurrah,
The ants go marching one by one, hur-
rah, hurrah,
The ants go marching one by one,
The little one stops to suck his thumb,
And they all go marching out in the big
parade.

The ants go marching two by two, hur-
rah, hurrah,
The ants go marching two by two, hur-
rah, hurrah,
The ants go marching two by two,
The little one stops to tie his shoe,
And they all go marching out in the big
parade.

The ants go marching three by three,
hurrah, hurrah,
The ants go marching three by three,
hurrah, hurrah,
The ants go marching three by three,
The little one stops to climb a tree,
And they all go marching out in the big
parade.

The ants go marching four by four,
hurrah, hurrah,
The ants go marching four by four,
hurrah, hurrah,
The ants go marching four by four,
The little one stops to sleep some more,
And they all go marching out in the big
parade.

The ants go marching five by five, hur-
rah, hurrah,
The ants go marching five by five, hur-
rah, hurrah,
The ants go marching five by five,
The little one stops to joke and jive,
And they all go marching out in the big
parade.

The ants go marching six by six, hur-
rah, hurrah,
The ants go marching six by six, hur-
rah, hurrah,
The ants go marching six by six,
The little one stops to do some tricks,
And they all go marching out in the big
parade.

The ants go marching seven by seven,
hurrah, hurrah,
The ants go marching seven by seven,
hurrah, hurrah,
The ants go marching seven by seven,
The little one stops to point to heaven,
And they all go marching out in the big
parade.

The ants go marching eight by eight,
hurrah, hurrah,
The ants go marching eight by eight,
hurrah, hurrah,
The ants go marching eight by eight,
The little one stops to shut the gate,
And they all go marching out in the big
parade.

The ants go marching nine by nine,
hurrah, hurrah,
The ants go marching nine by nine,
hurrah, hurrah,
The ants go marching nine by nine,
The little one stops to read a sign,
And they all go marching out in the big
parade.

The ants go marching ten by ten, hur-
rah, hurrah,
The ants go marching ten by ten, hur-
rah, hurrah,
The ants go marching ten by ten,
The little one stops to say "THE
END,"
And they all go marching out in the big
parade.

Baby Bumble Bee

To the tune of "Arkansas Traveller"

Baby Bumble Bee

Oh, I'm bringing home a baby bumble
bee,
Won't my mommy be so proud of me,
'Cause I'm bringing home a baby bum-
ble bee—
Buzzy, buzzy, buzzy—
(*spoken*) OOOOH, it bit me!

Oh, I'm bringing home a baby rattle-
snake,
Won't my mommy shi—ver and shake,
'Cause I'm bringing home a baby rattle-
snake—
Rattle, rattle, rattle—
(*spoken*) OOOOH, it bit me!

Oh, I'm bringing home a baby tur-tle,
Won't my mommy really pop her girdle,
'Cause I'm bringing home a baby
tur-tle—
Snappy, snappy, snappy—
(*spoken*) OOOOH, it bit me!

Oh, I'm bringing home a baby dinosaur,
Won't my mommy fall right through the
floor,
'Cause I'm bringing home a baby dino-
saur—
Gobble, gobble, gobble—
(*spoken*) OOOOH, it ate me!

The Grasshopper Song

The Grasshopper Song

The first grasshopper jumped right
over the second grasshopper's back.
Oh, the first grasshopper jumped right
over the second grasshopper's back.
The first grasshopper jumped right over
the second grasshopper's back.
Oh, the first grasshopper jumped right
over the second grasshopper's back.

Chorus

They were only playing leap frog,
They were only playing leap frog,
They were only playing leap frog,
In the springtime and the fall.

To the same tune:

The Flea Fly Song

One flea fly flew up the flu and
the other flea fly flew down.
Oh, one flea fly flew up the flu
and the other flea fly flew down.
Oh, one flea fly flew up the flu and
the other flea fly flew down.
Oh, one flea fly flew up the flu
and the other flea fly flew down.

Chorus

They were only playing flu fly,
They were only playing flu fly,
They were only playing flu fly
In the springtime and the fall.

There Was a Bee-Eye-Ee-Eye-Ee

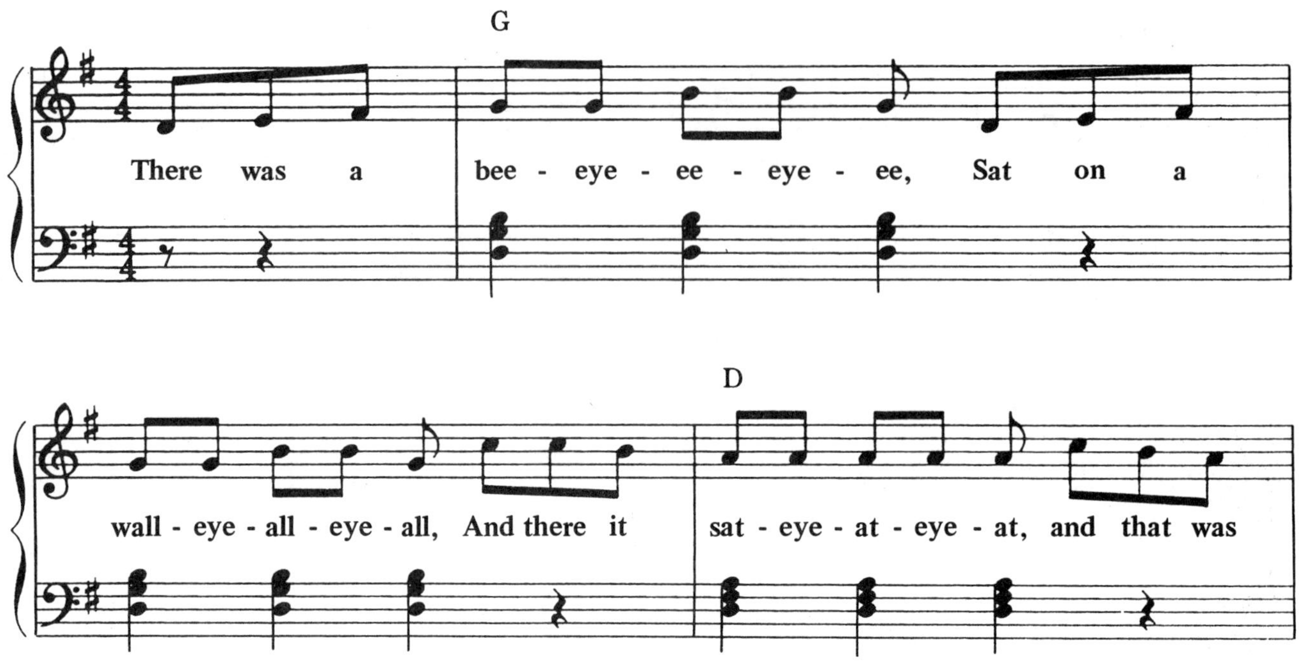

There was a bee-eye-ee-eye-ee,
Sat on a wall-eye-all-eye-all,
And there he sat-eye-at-eye-at,
And that was all-eye-all-eye-all.

Then came a boy-eye-oy-eye-oy,
Who had a stick-eye-ick-eye-ick,
And gave that bee-eye-ee-eye-ee
An awful lick-eye-ick-eye-ick.

And so that bee-eye-ee-eye-ee
Began to sting-eye-ing-eye-ing
And hurt that boy-eye-oy-eye-oy
Like anything-eye-ing-eye-ing!

And then that boy-eye-oy-eye-oy
Let out a yell-eye-ell-eye-ell
And told that bee-eye-ee-eye-ee
To go someplace I will not tell.

And then that bee-eye-ee-eye-ee
Gave one big cough-eye-off-eye-off,
And one last smile-eye-ile-eye-ile,
And he buzzed off-eye-off-eye-off.

ASK THE ANIMALS

Glunk, Glunk, Glunk

"Ba-rump," went the little green frog.
"Ba-rump," went the little green frog.
"Ba-rump," went the little green frog
one day,
And his eyes went, "Glunk, glunk, glunk!"

Where Is Your Goose?

Susie, oh, Susie,
Oh, where is your goose?
She's stuck in her nest
And I can't get her loose.

Johnny, oh, Johnny,
Oh, where is your cat?
He's lost in the cellar
And that—is that.

Freddie, oh, Freddie,
Oh, where is your hog?
He got cut in pork chops
And fed to the dog.

Cindy, oh, Cindy,
Where's your water snake?
He's hugged, and he's kissed,
And he's thrown in the lake.

Teddie, oh, Teddie,
Oh, where is your goat?
He's down at the pool
Where he's learning to float.

Linda, oh, Linda,
Oh, where is your pig?
He's gone to the store
To pick up a new wig.

Norman, oh, Norman,
Oh, where is your frog?
I bought him some sneakers
And taught him to jog.

Debbie, oh, Debbie,
Oh, where is your fish?
Right there in the oven—
He's baked in a dish.

Steven, oh, Steven,
Oh, where is your mouse?
He's eating Swiss cheese
In a trap in the house.

Shirley, oh, Shirley,
Oh, where is your duck?
He's off at the races
And trying his luck.

The Horse Went Around

To the tune of "Turkey in the Straw"

The Horse Went Around

Oh, the horse went around
With his foot off the ground.
Oh, the horse went around
With his foot off the ground.
Oh, the horse went around
With his foot off the ground.
Oh, the horse went around
With his foot off the ground.

Chorus

(spoken) Next verse
Same as the first.
A little bit louder
And a little bit worse.

Oh, the horse went around
With his foot off the ______ .
Oh, the horse went around
With his foot off the ______ .
Oh, the horse went around
With his foot off the ______ .
Oh, the horse went around
With his foot off the ______ .

Chorus

Oh, the horse went around
With his foot off ________ .
Oh, the horse went around
With his foot off ________ .
Oh, the horse went around
With his foot off ________ .
Oh, the horse went around
With his foot off ________ .

Chorus

Sing the song nine times, leaving out the last word each time, so that finally you're singing in total silence. After this, sing the entire song aloud once more.

Six Little Ducks

Six little ducks
That I once knew,
Fat ones, skinny ones,
Fair ones, too.
But the one little duck
With a feather on its back,
He led the others
With a quack, quack, quack.

Quack, quack, quack,
Quack, quack, quack.
He led the others
With a quack, quack, quack!

Down to the river they would go,
Wibble, wobble, wibble, wobble to and fro.

Six Little Ducks 

Home from the river they would come,
Wibble, wobble, wibble, wobble,
Right back home.

Quack, quack, quack,
Quack, quack, quack,
Right back home
With a quack, quack, quack!

● ● ● ● ● ● ● ● ● ● ● ● ● ●

Little Peter Rabbit

To the tune of "Battle Hymn of the Republic"

Little Peter Rabbit

Little Peter Rabbit had a fly upon his ear,
Little Peter Rabbit had a fly upon his ear,
Little Peter Rabbit had a fly upon his ear,
And he flicked it till it flew away!

Little Peter Rabbit had a fly upon his _____ ,
Little Peter Rabbit had a fly upon his _____ ,
Little Peter Rabbit had a fly upon his _____ ,
And he flicked it till it flew away.

Little Peter Rabbit had a _____ upon his _____ ,
Little Peter Rabbit had a _____ upon his _____ ,
Little Peter Rabbit had a _____ upon his _____ ,
And he flicked it till it flew away.

Little Peter _____ had a _____ upon his _____ ,
Little Peter _____ had a _____ upon his _____ ,
Little Peter _____ had a _____ upon his _____ ,
And he flicked it till it flew away.

Little _____ _____ had a _____ upon his _____ ,
Little _____ _____ had a _____ upon his _____ ,
Little _____ _____ had a _____ upon his _____ ,
And he flicked it till it flew away.

Three Green Speckled Frogs

Three green speckled frogs
Sat on a speckled log,
Eating some most delicious bugs,
(*spoken*) YUM YUM.

One jumped into the pool
Where it was nice and cool.
Then there were two green speckled frogs.

Two green speckled frogs
Sat on the speckled log,
Eating some most delicious bugs,
(*spoken*) YUM YUM.

One jumped into the pool
Where it was nice and cool.
Then there was one green speckled frog.

Three Green Speckled Frogs

One green speckled frog
Sat on a speckled log,
Eating some most delicious bugs,
(*spoken*) YUM YUM.
He jumped into the pool
Where it was nice and cool,
Then there were no green speckled frogs.

I Had a Rooster

This is an add-on song. Each time you sing a new verse, you add on all the animals that went before, ending with the little rooster.

I Had a Rooster

I Had a Rooster

I had a rooster and the rooster pleased
me,
I fed my rooster on a greenberry tree.
The little rooster went, "Cock-a-doodle
doo,
Dee doodle-dee, doodle-dee, doodle-dee
doo."

I had a cat and the cat pleased me,
I fed my cat on a greenberry tree.
The little cat went, (*spoken*), "Meow,
meow,"
The little rooster went, "Cock-a-doodle
doo,
Dee doodle-dee, doodle-dee, doodle-dee
doo."

Go on to more verses:

I had a pig ("oink, oink, oink")
I had a cow ("mooo, mooo")
I had a duck ("quack, quack, quack")
I had a lion ("roar, roar")
I had a baby ("waagh, waagh")

You don't have to stick with animals or humans. You can make up your own verses using anything you want. You could try:

clocks ("tick, tick-tock")
trains ("choo, choo, choo")
cars ("beep, beep, beep")
musical instruments such as horns ("toot, toot, toot") or guitars ("plunk, plunk, plunk")
or even computers ("blip, blip, blip")

and you can vary the sound effects.

SNACKTIME!

The Duchess at Tea

I sat next to the Duchess at tea.
It was just as I thought it would be.
Her rum-bl-ings ab-dom-in-al
Were sim-pl-y phen-om-en-al,
Everyone thought it was me!

The Prune Song

The Quartermaster Corps

Oh, it's beans, beans, beans,
That turn us into fiends
In the corps, in the corps.
Oh, it's beans, beans, beans,
That turn us into fiends,
In the Quartermaster Corps.

Chorus

Mine eyes are dim;
I cannot see.
I have not brought my specs with me.

Oh, it's soup, soup, soup,
That knocks you for a loop
In the corps, in the corps,
Oh, it's soup, soup, soup
That knocks you for a loop
In the Quartermaster Corps.

Chorus

Oh, it's cheese, cheese, cheese,
That brings you to your knees
In the corps, in the corps. (*Repeat*)

Chorus

Oh, it's cake, cake, cake,
That makes your stomach ache
In the corps, in the corps. (*Repeat*)

Chorus

Oh, it's pie, pie, pie,
That hits you in the eye
In the corps, in the corps. (*Repeat*)

Chorus

Oh, it's meat, meat, meat,
That isn't fit to eat
In the corps, in the corps. (*Repeat*)

Chorus

Oh, it's peas, peas, peas,
That make you want to sneeze
In the corps, in the corps. (*Repeat*)

Chorus

Oh, it's stew, stew, stew,
That turns you black and blue
In the corps, in the corps. (*Repeat*)

Chorus

Oh, it's bread, bread, bread,
Sits in your gut like lead
In the corps, in the corps. (*Repeat*)

Chorus

Oh, it's pears, pears, pears,
That give you curly hairs
In the corps, in the corps. (*Repeat*)

Chorus

The Quartermaster Corps

The Peanut Butter Song

CHORUS

You take the peanut butter
And you spread it, you spread it.
You take the peanut butter
And you spread it, you spread it.

Chorus

Then you take the grapes
and you squish 'em, you squish 'em.
Then you take the grapes
And you squish 'em, you squish 'em.

Chorus

Then you take the jelly
And you spread it, you spread it.
Then you take the jelly
And you spread it, you spread it.

You take the peanut butter and jelly
And put them together, put them together.
You take the peanut butter and jelly
And put them together, put them together.

Chorus

Then you take that knife
And you cut it, you cut it,
Then you take that knife
And you cut it, you cut it.

Chorus

Then you take the sandwich
And you eat it, you eat it.
Then you take the sandwich
And you eat it, you eat it.

The Peanut Butter Song

Hum the chorus three or four or five times more and more quietly, until fadeout, chewing.

• • • • • • • • • • • • • •

On Top of My Pizza

On top of my pizza—
All covered with sauce—
Could not find the mushrooms,
I think they got lost.

I looked in the closet,
I looked in the sink,
I looked in the cup that
Held my cola drink.

I looked in the saucepan,
Right under the lid,
No matter where I looked,
Those mushrooms stayed hid.

Next time you make pizza,
I'm begging you, please,
Do not give me mushrooms,
But just plain old cheese.

The Swiss Cheese Song

There once was a woman who gobbled
Swiss cheese,
Gobbled Swiss cheese, gobbled Swiss
cheese,
And one day she woke up with holes in
her knees,
Woke up with holes in her knees. . . .

This woman cried, "Help me, oh, what
can I do?
What can I do? What can I do?
When I look at my knees I see sky
shining through.
Now I see sky shining through."

The Swiss Cheese Song

She ran to the doctor who answered
with ease,
Answered with ease, answered with
ease,
"Just swallow some tiddlywinks.
They'll fill up your knees.
Tiddlywinks will fill up your knees."

She salted some tiddlywinks and gob-
bled down lots,
Gobbled down lots, gobbled down lots.
Now 'stead of holes, she's got green
polka dots,
Now she's got green polka dots.

Three Ways to Get Peanut Butter Off the Roof of Your Mouth

There are three ways to get peanut
butter off the roof of your
mouth.
One way is to shake your head back
and forth
(*shake head vigorously*).
If that doesn't work
you could kind of whistle
(*whistle*).

If this doesn't work, you could scrape it
off with your first finger
(*scrape it off*).

There are three ways to get peanut
butter off your finger.
One way is to shake it off
(*shake finger vigorously*).
Another way is to blow it off
(*try that*).
If that doesn't work, you can scrape it
off with your two front teeth
(*do it*).

There are three ways to get peanut
butter off the roof of your
mouth (*and so on*).

Gum Song

Chomp chomp, nibble nibble, yum,
yum, yum,
I love to chew on my chewing gum.
My chewing gum's so good and sweet,
It makes me happy from my head to my
feet.

I love to pull my gum out far
And pluck it like a big guitar.
I wind it around my thumb with care,
'Cause nobody likes it when it gets in
your hair.

Blowing a bubble's mighty tough,
You've got to stick your tongue out
enough.
Now I'm ready, just look at me
And I'll blow you a bubble as big as a
tree.

Sometimes when I'm chewing gum
I make it flat with the top of my tongue.
I make it flat, then I take it out
And it makes a map of the top of my
mouth.

My gum makes pops and cracks and
clicks
Against my teeth and against my lips.
When I'm all alone, no one else around,
I love to hear that chewing gum sound.

Chomp chomp, nibble nibble, yum,
yum, yum,
I love to chew on my chewing gum.
My chewing gum's so good and sweet,
It makes me happy from my head to my
feet.

Birds in the Wilderness

Here we sit like birds in the wilderness,
Birds in the wilderness,
Birds in the wilderness,
Here we sit like birds in the wilderness,
Waiting for our food.

Here we sit like birds in the wilderness,
Birds in the wilderness,
Birds in the wilderness,
Here we sit like birds in the wilderness,
Waiting for our soup.

Here we sit like birds in the wilderness,
Birds in the wilderness,
Birds in the wilderness,
Here we sit like birds in the wilderness,
Waiting for our bread.

Here we sit like birds in the wilderness,
Birds in the wilderness,
Birds in the wilderness,
Here we sit like birds in the wilderness,
Waiting for our meat.

Here we sit like birds in the wilderness,
Birds in the wilderness,
Birds in the wilderness,
Here we sit like birds in the wilderness,
Waiting for dessert.

I Want a Chocolate Malted (Round)

The music for this song is actually based on the Grand Fugue from Bach's Toccata in G Minor. It makes a yummy round.

I want—
I want a malted,
I want a chocolate malted,
I want a chocolate malted.

KOOKY CHARACTERS

Old Mother Leary

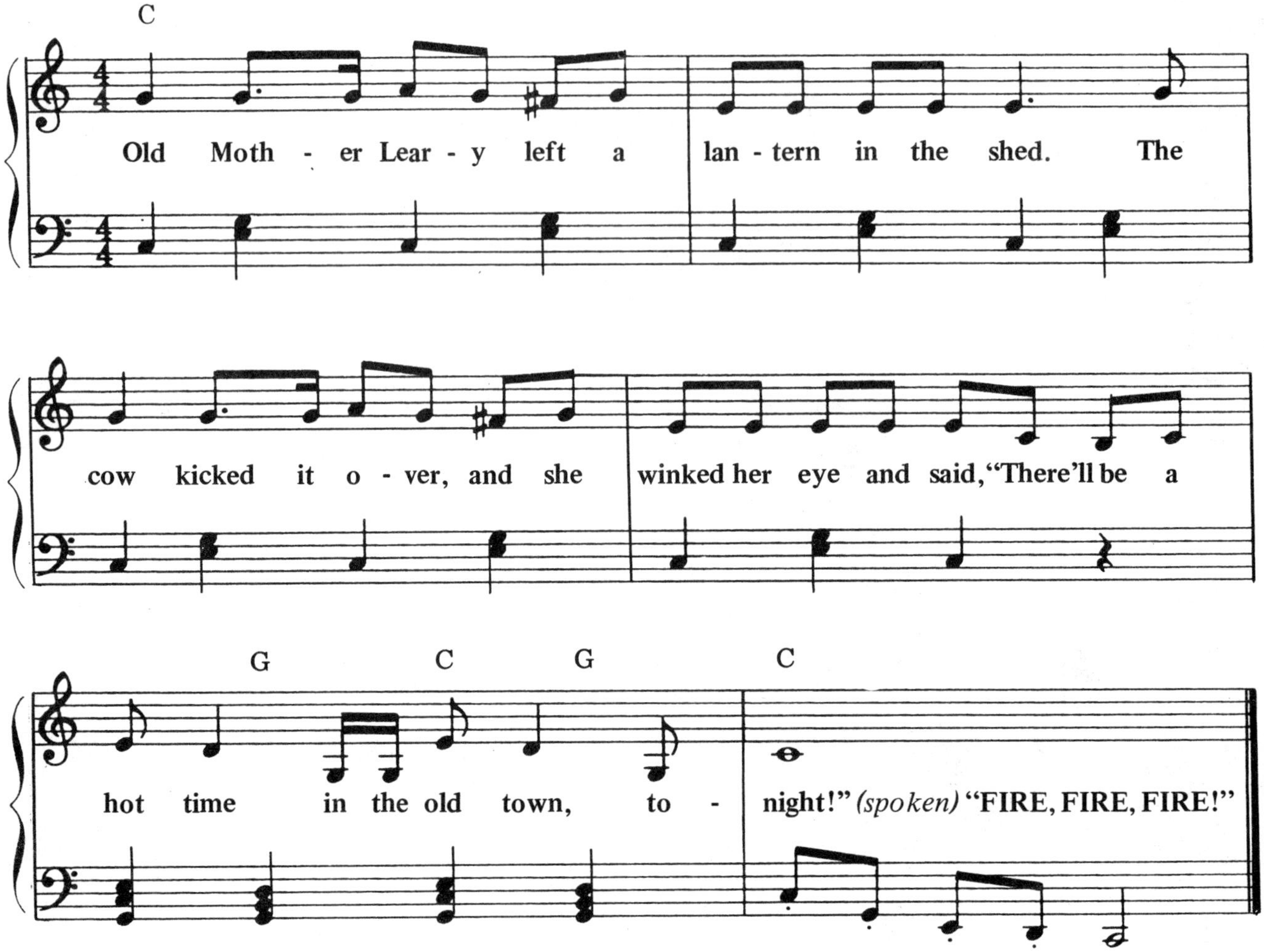

Old Mother Leary left a lantern in the
shed.
The cow kicked it over, and she winked
her eye and said,
"There'll be a hot time in the old town,
tonight."

(*spoken*) "FIRE, FIRE, FIRE!"

Dirty Bill

I know a man named Dirty Bill,
Lives in a house on Garbage Hill,
Never took a bath and never will.
Oigh, foigh, Dirty Bill!

Clementine

G
In a cav - ern, in a can - yon, ex - ca - vat - ing for a
D D7 G D
mine, Lived a min - er, for - ty - nin - er, And his daugh - ter, Cle - men -
G CHORUS
tine. Oh, my dar - ling, oh, my dar - ling, Oh, my dar - ling Cle - men -
D D7 G D G
tine, You are lost and gone for - ev - er, Dread-ful sor - ry, Cle - men - tine.

Clementine

In a cavern, in a canyon,
Excavating for a mine,
Lived a miner forty-niner
And his daughter, Clementine.

Chorus
Oh, my darling, oh, my darling,
Oh, my darling Clementine,
You are lost and gone forever,
Dreadful sorry, Clementine.

Light she was and like a fairy,
And her shoes were number nine,
Herring boxes without topses,
Sandals were for Clementine.

Chorus

Drove her ducklings to the water,
Every morning just at nine,
Hit her foot against a splinter,
Fell into the foaming brine.

Chorus

Ruby lips above the water,
Blowing bubbles soft and fine,
But alas, I was no swimmer
So I lost my Clementine.

Chorus

Then the miner, forty-niner,
Soon began to peak and pine,
Thought he oughta join his daughter,
Now he's with his Clementine.

Chorus

There's a churchyard on the hillside,
Where the flowers grow and twine,
There grow roses, 'mongst the posies,
Fertilized by Clementine.

Chorus

In my dreams she still doth haunt me,
Robed in garlands soaked in brine,
Though in life I used to hug her,
Now she's dead, I draw the line.

Chorus

Now you scouts may learn the moral
Of this little tale of mine,
Artificial respiration
Would have saved my Clementine.

Chorus

How I missed her, how I missed her,
How I missed my Clementine,
Till I kissed her little sister,
And forgot my Clementine.

Chorus

Sweet Rosie O'Grady

Arabella Miller

Little Arabella Miller
Found a woolly caterpillar.
First it crawled upon her mother,
Then upon her little brother.
They said, "Arabella Miller,
Take away your caterpillar!"

Arabella did not take it.
She decided to forsake it.
So it crawled up on the tree
And fell down on you and me.
Please, dear Arabella Miller,
Take away your caterpillar!

Old Joe Clarke

Old Joe Clarke's a fine old man,
Tell you the reason why.
He keeps good candy round his house
And lots of apple pie.

Chorus
Fare ye well, Old Joe Clarke,
Fare ye well, I say,
Fare ye well, Old Joe Clarke,
I'm a-goin' away.

Old Joe Clarke

Old Joe Clarke had a house
Fifteen stories high,
And every story in that house
Was filled with chicken pie.

Chorus

I went down to Old Joe's house,
Never been there before.
He slept on the feather bed
And I slept on the floor.

Chorus

Old Joe Clarke had a cow,
She was long as a rail.
It took a blackbird one whole day
To fly from head to tail!

Chorus

Old Joe Clarke had a mule,
His name was Morgan Brown.
And every tooth in that mule's head
Was sixteen inches round.

Chorus

Old Joe Clarke had a cat—
She was fat and mean.
She stuck her head in the buttermilk jar
And washed her whiskers clean.

Chorus

I went down to Old Joe's house—
He invited me to supper.
I stubbed my toe on the table leg
And stuck my nose in the butter.

Chorus

Old Mrs. Lazibones

Old Mrs. Lazibones

Old Mrs. Lazibones
And her dirty daughter
Never used soap
And never used water.

Chorus Higgledy piggledy cowpat,
What d'you think of that?

Daisies from their fingernails,
Birds' nests in their hair-O,
Dandelions from their ears,
What a dirty pair-O!

Chorus

Came a prince who sought a bride,
Riding past their doorstep,
"Quick," said Mrs. Lazibones.
"Girl, under the water tap."

Chorus

Washed her up and washed her down,
Then she washed her sideways,
But the prince was far, far away,
He'd ridden off on the highways.

Chorus

Christopher McCracken

To the tune of "Battle Hymn of the Republic"

Christopher McCracken

Christopher McCracken went a-fishing
for some crabs,
Christopher McCracken went a-fishing
for some crabs,
Christopher McCracken went a-fishing
for some crabs,
But he didn't catch a (*clap, clap*) crab.

Oh, all he caught was some old virus,
All he caught was some old virus,
All he caught was some old virus,
But he didn't catch a (*clap, clap*) crab.

Lulabel

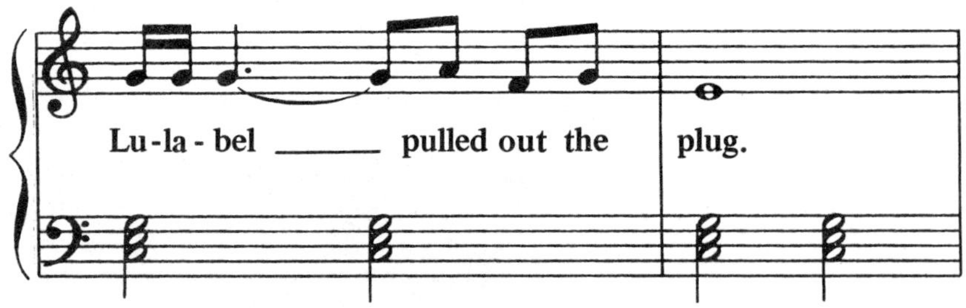

(Spoken in falsetto voice)

OH MY GOODNESS!
OH MY SOUL!
THERE GOES LULABEL
DOWN THE HOLE!

THE BEST OF THE BEASTS

Five Little Monkeys

Five little monkeys walked along the shore,
One went sailing,
Then there were four.

Four little monkeys climbed up a tree,
One of them tumbled down,
Then there were three.

Three little monkeys found a pot of glue,
One got stuck in it,
Then there were two.

Two little monkeys found a raisin bun,
One ran away with it,
Then there was one.

One little monkey, red in the face,
They trained him as an astronaut
And sent him out in space.

The Little Skunk Hole

Oh, I stuck my head
In the little skunk hole,
And the little skunk said,
"Well, bless my soul!
Take it out! Take it out! Take it out!
TAKE IT OUT!
REMOVE IT!"

Well, I didn't take it out,
And the little skunk said,
"If you don't take it out,
You'll wish you were dead.
Take it out! Take it out! Take it out!
(*holding nose*) Pee-yoo! I removed it
(*spoken*) TOOOO LATE!!!!!!!!!!

The Smile on the Crocodile

She sailed away on a sunny summer day
On the back of a crocodile.
''You see,'' said she,
''He's as tame as he can be—
I'll ride him down the Nile.''

The Smile on the Crocodile

The croc winked his eye
As she bade them all good-bye,
Wearing a happy smile.
At the end of the ride,
The lady was inside
And the smile on the crocodile!

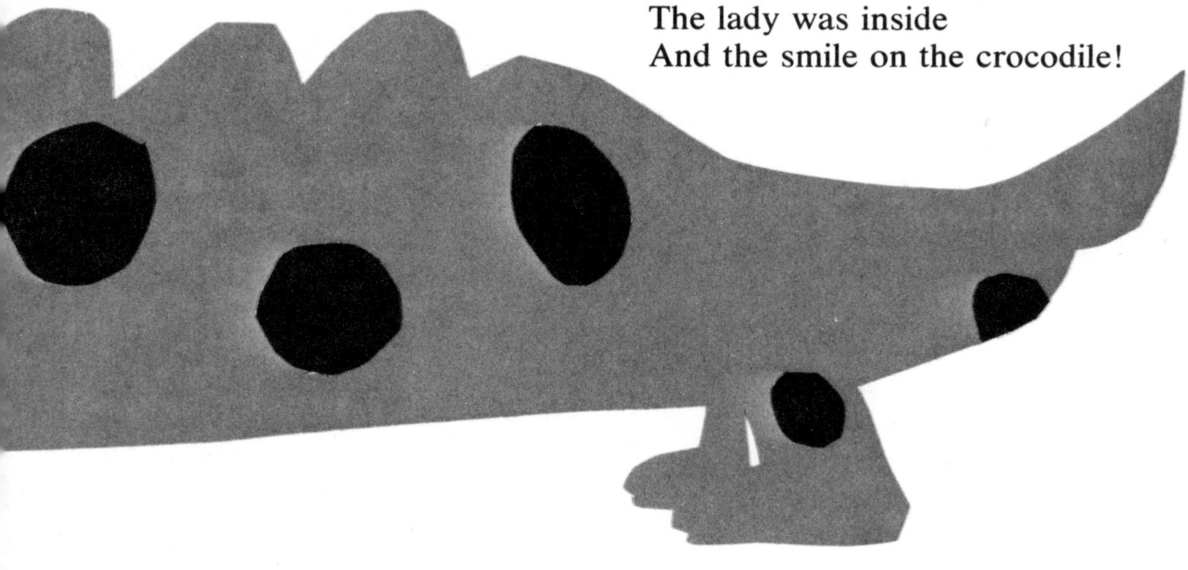

The Bear Song

The other day
  (the other day)
I saw a bear
  (I saw a bear),
A great big bear
  (a great big bear)
A-way up there
  (a-way up there),
The other day I saw a bear,
A great big bear a-way up there.

He looked at me
  (he looked at me),
I looked at him
  (I looked at him),
He sized up me
  (he sized up me),
I sized up him
  (I sized up him),
He looked at me, I looked at him,
He sized up me, I sized up him.

The Bear Song

He said to me
 (he said to me),
"Why don't you run?
 (Why don't you run?)
I see you ain't
 (I see you ain't)
Got any gun."
 (got any gun)
He said to me, "Why don't you run?
I see you ain't got any gun."

And so I ran
 (and so I ran)
Away from there
 (away from there),
And right behind
 (and right behind)
Me was that bear
 (me was that bear),
And so I ran away from there,
And right behind me was that bear.

In front of me
 (in front of me)
There was a tree
 (there was a tree),
A great big tree
 (a great big tree),
Oh, golly gee
 (oh, golly gee),
In front of me there was a tree,
A great big tree, oh, golly gee.

The nearest branch
 (the nearest branch)
Was ten feet up
 (was ten feet up),
I had to jump
 (I had to jump)
And trust my luck
 (and trust my luck),
The nearest branch was ten feet up,
I had to jump and trust my luck.

And so I jumped
 (and so I jumped)
Into the air
 (into the air),
And missed that branch
 (and missed that branch)
Away up there
 (away up there),
And so I jumped into the air,
And missed that branch away up there.

Now don't you fret
 (now don't you fret)
And don't you frown
 (and don't you frown),
I caught that branch
 (I caught that branch)
On the way back down
 (on the way back down)
Now don't you fret and don't you frown
I caught that branch on the way back down.

That's all there is
 (that's all there is)
There ain't no more
 (there ain't no more),
Until I meet
 (until I meet)
That bear once more
 (that bear once more),
That's all there is, there ain't no more,
Until I meet that bear once more.

The end the end
 (the end the end)
The end the end
 (the end the end),
The end the end
 (the end the end)
The end the end
 (the end the end),
The end the end the end the end,
This time it really is the end.

Pop Goes the Weasel!

All around the cobbler's bench,
The monkey chased the weasel.
The monkey thought 'twas all in fun,
Pop—goes the weasel!
Johnny's got the whooping cough
And Mary's got the measles,
That's the way the money goes,
Pop—goes the weasel!

A penny for a spool of thread,
A penny for a needle,
That's the way the money goes,
Pop—goes the weasel!
You may try to sew and sew
And never make anything regal
So roll it up and let it go,
Pop—goes the weasel!

Pop Goes the Weasel!

A painter would his lover to paint,
He stood before the easel.
The monkey jumped all over the paint,
Pop—goes the weasel!
When his sweetheart she did laugh,
His temper got so lethal,
He tore the painting up in half,
Pop—goes the weasel!

My son and I went to the fair,
We saw a lot of people.
We spent a lot of money there,
Pop—goes the weasel!
I got sick from all the sun,
My sonny boy got the measles.
Still we had a lot of fun,
Pop—goes the weasel!

I climbed up and down the coast
To find a golden eagle.
I climbed the rocks and thought I was close,
Pop—goes the weasel!
But, alas, I lost my way,
Saw nothing but a seagull,
I tore my pants and killed the day,
Pop—goes the weasel!

I went to the grocery store,
I thought a little cheese'll
Be good to catch a mouse on the floor,
Pop—goes the weasel!
But the mouse was very bright
He wasn't a mouse to wheedle,
He took the cheese and said, "Good-night,"
Pop—goes the weasel!

Up and down the City Road,
In and out the Eagle,
That's the way the money goes,
Pop—goes the weasel!
Half a pound of tuppenny rice,
Half a pound of treacle,
Mix it up and make it nice,
Pop—goes the weasel!

Every night when I go out,
The monkey's on the table,
Take a stick and knock it off,
Pop—goes the weasel!
Put some pepper on its nose,
And you'll make it sneeze-l,
Catch it fast before it snaps—
Pop—goes the weasel!

A penny for a cotton ball,
A penny for a needle,
That's the way the money goes,
Pop—goes the weasel!
If you want to buy a pig,
Buy a pig with hairs on,
Every hair a penny a pair,
Pop—goes the weasel!

All around the cobbler's bench,
The monkey chased the weasel.
The monkey thought 'twas all in fun,
Pop—goes the weasel!
I've no time to wait and sigh,
I've no time to tease-l,
Kiss me quick—I'm off—goodbye!
Pop—goes the weasel!

Fuzzy Wuzzy

Fuzzy Wuzzy was a bear,
Fuzzy Wuzzy had no hair.
Fuzzy Wuzzy wasn't fuzzy,
No, by gosh, he wasn't, wuzz he?

COMPLETELY CRAZY

I Wish I Was

F
C
3
I wish I was a ra-na-sa-sor-i-us, a re-pa-pa-
F
tame-aye-ee ha-ha-ha-ha. But since I am not And nev-er can
C7
hope to be a ra-na-sa-sor-i-us, a re-pa-pa-
F
Gm
tame-eye-ee, I'm a June bug, I'm a tur-tle, And I
C7
love to hit my head a-gainst the wall. Click Click.
(Click your tongue twice)

I Wish I Was

I wish I was
a ranasasorius,
a re-papa-tame-eye-ee—
ha-ha-ha-ha.
But since I am not
And never can hope to be
a ranasasorius,
a re-papa-tame-eye-ee—
I'm a June bug,
I'm a turtle,
And I love to hit my head against the wall.
Click Click
(*click your tongue twice*)

The Alphabet Song

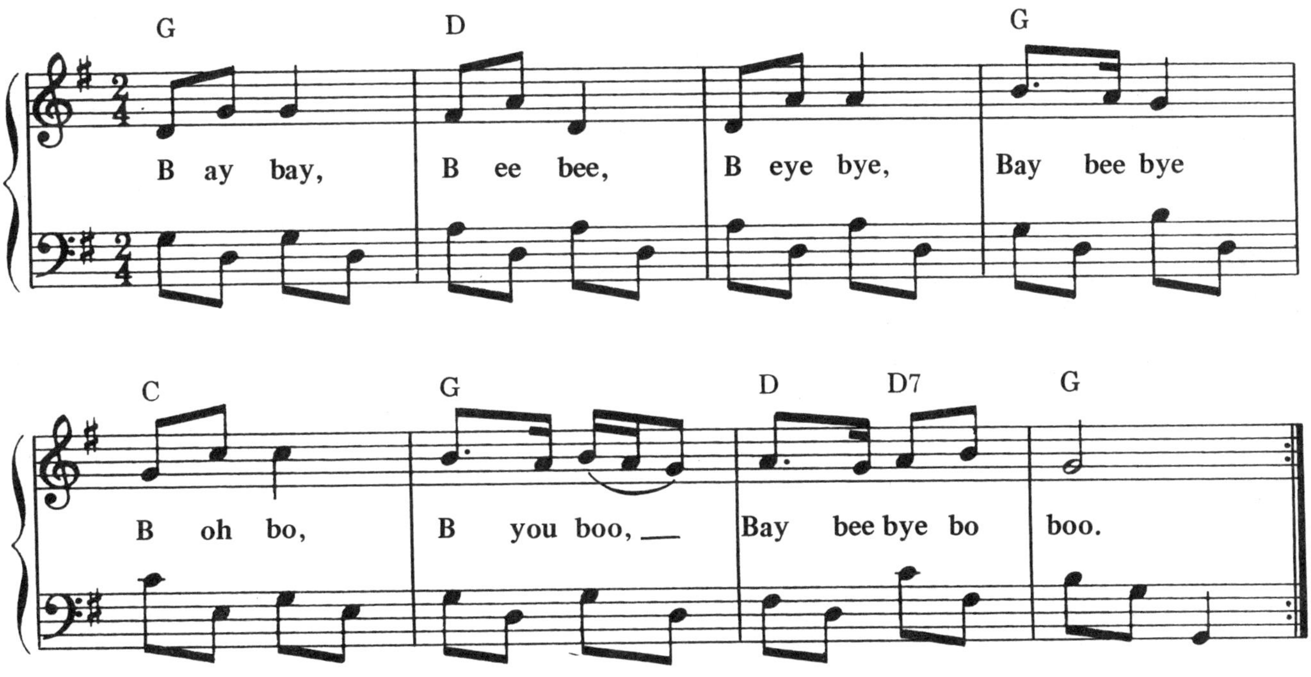

B	ay	bay		
B	ee	bee		
B	eye	bye		
Bay	bee	bye		
B	oh	bo		
Bay	bee	bye	bo	
B	you	boo		
Bay	bee	bye	bo	boo.

C	ay	say		
C	ee	see		
C	eye	sigh		
Say	see	sigh		
C	oh	so		
Say	see	sigh	so	
C	you	sue		
Say	see	sigh	so	sue.

(*And so on.*)

Let's Go Bowling in Bowling Green

To the tune of "Here We Go Round the Mulberry Bush"

Let's go bowling in Bowling Green,
In Bowling Green, in Bowling Green,
Let's go bowling in Bowling Green,
So early in the morning.

(*spoken*) We can't go bowling in Bowling Green,
Why can't we go bowling in Bowling Green?
Because of the king.
What king?
Father of the prince.
What prince?
Paw prints—
Handprints—
Fingerprints—
Blueprints—
(*whistle and beckon with finger*) Here, Prince, Prince, Prince!

The moral of this story is:
NEVER CONFUSE ASTHMA (wheeze)—
WITH PASSION (sigh)!

A Sailor Went to Sea Sea Sea

A sailor went to sea sea sea
To see what he could see see see,
But all that he could see see see
Was the bottom of the deep blue sea
sea sea.

Oh, Helen had a steamboat,
The steamboat had a bell,
When Helen went to heaven
The steamboat went to —

Hello, operator,
Just give me number 9.
If the line is busy
I'll kick your big —

Behind the old piano,
There was a piece of glass,
Helen slipped upon it
And hurt her little —

Ask me for a muffin,
I'll give you some old bread
And if you do not like it,
Just go and soak your head.

Do Your Ears Hang Low?

Do your ears hang low?
Do they wobble to and fro?
Can you tie them in a knot?
Can you tie them in a bow?
Can you toss them over your shoulder
Like a continental soldier?
Do your ears—hang—low?

Yes, my ears hang low.
They can wobble to and fro,
I can tie them in a knot,
I can tie them in a bow,
I can toss them over my shoulder
Like a continental soldier.
Yes, my ears—hang—low.

I'm a Nut

I'm wild about horns on automobiles
That go, "whah ah ah ah ah ah ah ah."
I'm a nut!—Click click—
I'm a pest—Click click—
And the thing I love the best— (*start again.*)

Reuben, Reuben

Reuben, Reuben, I've been thinking,
What the heck have you been drinking?
Looks like water, tastes like wine—
Oh, my gosh, it's turpentine.

I've got a dog; his name is Rover,
He's a very clever pup.
He will stand upon his hind legs,
If you hold his front legs up.

Reuben, Reuben, I've been thinking,
What a silly world this would be,
If the monkeys lived in houses
and we swung from tree to tree.

There's no need to light a night light
On a light night like tonight—
For a night light's light is slight light
When the moonlight's white and bright.

Reuben, Reuben, I've been thinking,
What a funny world this would be,
If jet planes lived in apartments
And we flew across the sea.

I Am Slowly Going Crazy

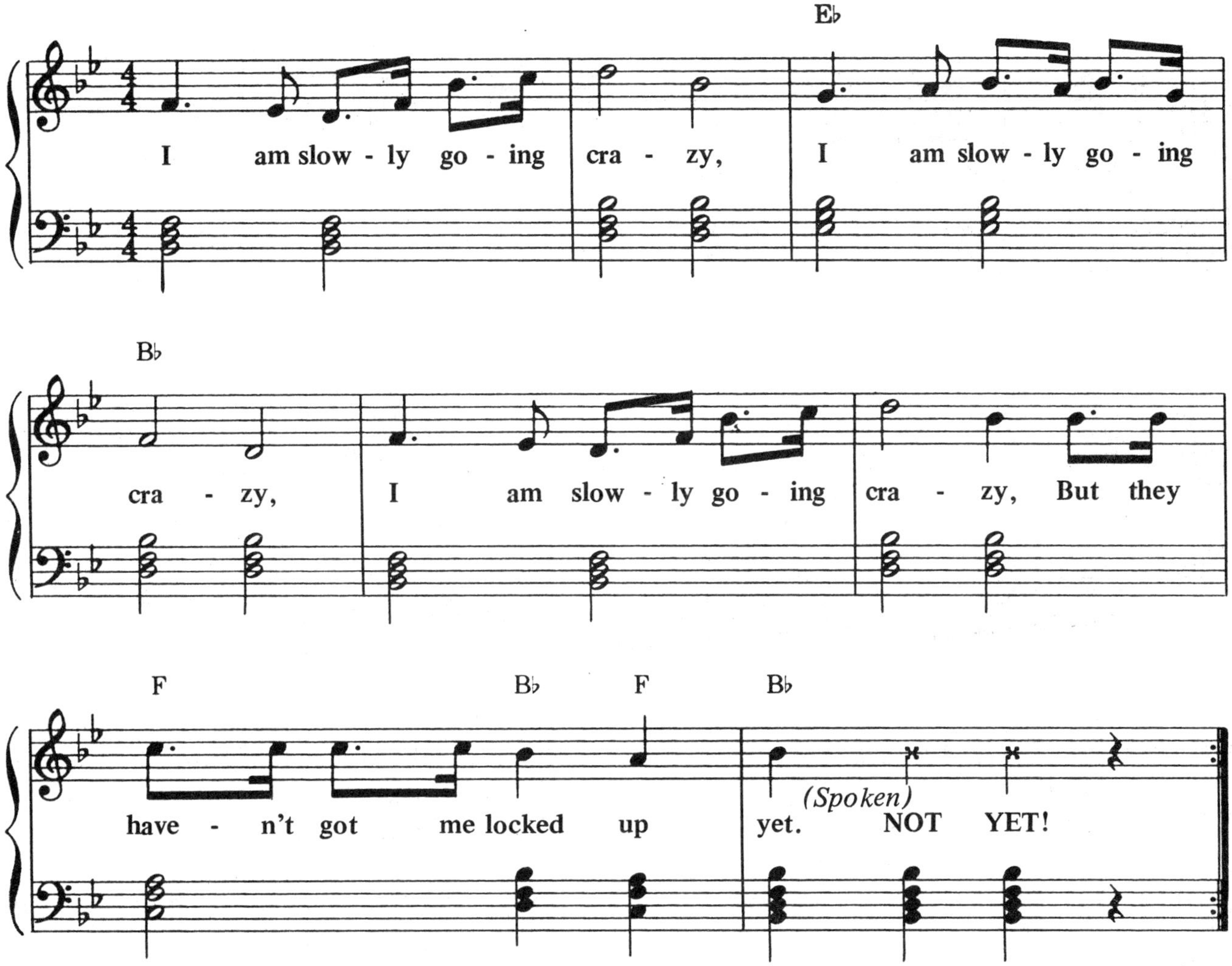

Chorus

I am slowly going crazy,
I am slowly going crazy,
I am slowly going crazy,
But they haven't got me locked up yet!
(*spoken*) NOT YET!

It was midnight on the ocean,
Not a taxi in sight.
The sun was shining brightly,
And it rained all day that night.

Chorus

Please don't ask me any questions,
I will make no more suggestions.
Please don't ask me any questions,
And I'll tell you no more lies.

Chorus

Poor Roger Is Dead and Gone to His Grave

Poor Roger is dead and gone to his grave,
Hi-ho, gone to his grave.

There grew an old apple tree over his head,
Hi-ho, over his head.

The apples were ripe and ready to fall,
Hi-ho, ready to fall.

There came an old woman, a-picking them up,
Hi-ho, a-picking them up.

Old Roger jumped up and he gave her a knock,
Hi-ho, gave her a knock.

Which made the old woman go clippety-clop,
Hi-ho, clippety-clop.

The saddle and bridle, they lie on the shelf,
Hi-ho, lie on the shelf.

If you want any more, you can sing it yourself,
Hi-ho, sing it yourself!

PURE SILLINESS

Ninety-nine Miles from Home

Oh, I'm ninety-nine miles from home,
I'm ninety-nine miles from home.
I walk a while, and rest a while,
I'm ninety-nine miles from home.

Oh, I'm ninety-eight miles from home,
I'm ninety-eight miles from home.
I walk a while, and rest a while,
I'm ninety-eight miles from home.

(*And so on . . . .*)

We Don't Want to Go Home

Ten more days of vacation,
Then we go back to the station,
Back to civilization—
We don't want to go home.

We don't want to go home,
We don't want to go home,
We don't want to go home,
We want to stay right here!

Start with ten days of vacation. Then each day subtract one and sing the new number of days left. Finally:

No more days of vacation,
We have to go back to the station,
Back to civilization—
Now we have to go home.

Around the Corner

Around the corner, and under a tree,
A sergeant major once said to me,
"Who would marry you?
I would like to know,
For every time I look at your face,
It makes me want to go
Around the corner," and under a tree

(*and on and on and on*).

Three Little Witches

One little—
Two little—
Three little witches,
Flying over haystacks,
Jumping over ditches.
One little—
Two little—
Three little witches—
HAPPY HALLOWEEN!

One little—
Two little—
Three little witches,
Flew over the fence and
Ripped their britches,
Sewed them
Up with fifty stitches—
HAPPY HALLOWEEN!

Catch a Wiffer Woffer

Catch a Wiffer Woffer

Oh, I'm walkin' round the corner
Doing little harm,
Along comes a policeman
And grabs me by the arm.

Oh, he walks me round the corner,
Rings a little bell,
Along comes a wagon,
And knocks me in a cell.

Chorus

I'm singin' eenie meenie and a miney
moh,
Catch a wiffer woffer by the toe,
And if it hollers, hollers, hollers,
Let it go, I'm singin'
Eenie meenie and a miney moh.

Oh, five o'clock in the morning
I looked up on the wall—
The roaches and the bedbugs
Were having a game of ball.

Oh, the score was six to nothing,
The roaches were ahead—
The bedbugs hit a home run
And knocked me out of bed.

Chorus

Oh, six o'clock in the morning
The jailer comes around,
A piece of bread and coffee
That weighs a half a pound.

Oh, the coffee tastes like tobacco juice,
The bread is hard and stale,
But that's the way they treat the bums
In New York County Jail.

Chorus

I went downtown for breakfast
I ordered ham and eggs.
I ate so many pickles,
The juice ran down my legs.

I fell into a sewer
And that is where I died.
They did not call it murder—
They called it sewer-cide.

Chorus

The Billboard Song

As I was walking down the street
One dark and dismal day,
I came upon a billboard
And much to my dismay,
The sign was torn and tattered
From a storm the night before.
The wind and rain had done its job
And this is what I saw:

The Billboard Song

Smoke Coca-Cola cigarettes,
Chew Wrigley-Spearmint beer,
And Kennel Ration Dog Food
Makes your wife's complexion clear.
Oh, simonize your baby,
With a Hershey's candy bar,
And Texaco's the beauty cream
That's used by every star.

Please take your next vacation
In a brand new Frigidaire.
And learn to play piano
In your winter underwear.
The doctors say that babies
Should smoke till they are three,
And people in the cities
Ought to bathe in Lipton's Tea—
with flow-through tea bags!

Mud, Mud, Glorious Mud

Mud, mud, glorious mud,
Nothing quite like it for cooling your blood.
Follow me, follow,
Down to the hollow,
Where we will wallow
In glorious mud.

One Bottle Pop

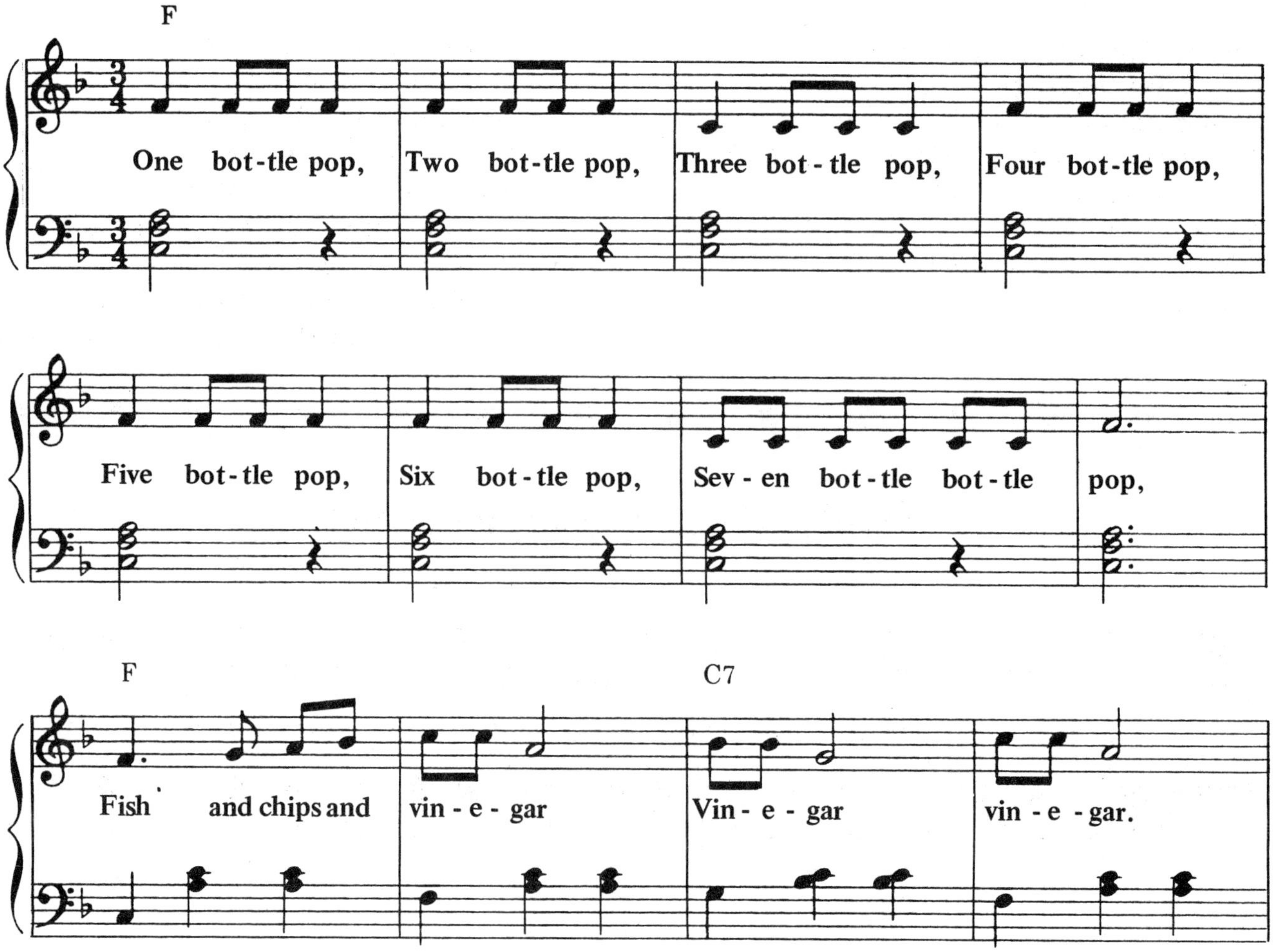

One bottle pop,
Two bottle pop,
Three bottle pop,
Four bottle pop,
Five bottle pop,
Six bottle pop,
Seven bottle bottle pop,

Fish and chips and vinegar,
Vinegar, vinegar.
Fish and chips and vinegar.
Pepper pepper pepper salt.

One Bottle Pop

Don't throw your trash in my back yard,
My back yard, my back yard
Don't throw your trash in my back yard
My back yard's full!

The Walloping Windowblind

A capital ship for an ocean trip
Was the Walloping Windowblind.
No wind that blew
Dismayed her crew
Nor troubled the captain's mind.
The man at the wheel
Was made to feel
Contempt for the wildest blow-oh-oh,
Though it often appeared
When the gale had cleared
That he'd been in his bunk below.

Chorus

Then blow ye winds heigh-ho
A-roving I will go.
I'll stay no more
On England's shore
So let the music play-ay-ay—
I'm off on the morning train
I'll sail the raging main.
I'm off to my love
With a boxing glove
Ten thousand miles away.

The captain's mate was very sedate,
Yet fond of amusement, too.
He played hopscotch
With the starboard watch,
While the captain tickled the crew.
The gunner we had was apparently
mad,
For he sat on the after rail-ail-ail—
And fired salutes with the captain's
boots
In the teeth of the raging gale.

Chorus

The captain sat on the commodore's hat
And dined in a royal way
On snails and eels and cockatoo heels
And pickled figs each day.
The cook was new and burned the
stew,
So the diet he served the crew
Was a couple of tons of hot cross buns
Served up with sugar and glue.

Chorus

The Walloping Windowblind

The Walloping Windowblind

CAN YOU TOP THIS?

There Were Three Jolly Fishermen

There were three jolly fishermen,
There were three jolly fishermen,
Fisher, fisher, men, men, men.
Fisher, fisher, men, men, men.
There were three jolly fishermen.

The first one's name was Abraham.
The first one's name was Abraham.
Abra, Abra, ham, ham, ham.
Abra, Abra, ham, ham, ham.
The first one's name was Abraham.

The next one's name was Isaac.
The next one's name was Isaac.
I, I, zic, zic, zic.
I, I, zic, zic, zic.
The next one's name was Isaac.

The third one's name was Jacob.
The third one's name was Jacob.
Jay, Jay, cub, cub, cub.
Jay, Jay, cub, cub, cub.
The third one's name was Jacob.

They all sailed up to Jericho.
They all sailed up to Jericho.
Jerry, Jerry, co, co, co.
Jerry, Jerry, co, co, co.
They all sailed up to Jericho.

They should have gone to Amsterdam.
They should have gone to Amsterdam.
Amster, Amster, sh, sh, sh.
Amster, Amster, sh, sh, sh.
Mustn't say that naughty word.

There Were Three Jolly Fishermen

I think I'll say it anyway.
I think I'll say it anyway.
Any, any, way, way, way.
Any, any, way, way, way.
I think I'll say it anyway.

They should have gone to Amsterdam.
They should have gone to Amsterdam.
Amster, Amster, dam, dam, dam.
Amster, Amster, dam, dam, dam.
They should have gone to Amsterdam.

The Old Family Toothbrush

To the tune of "The Old Oaken Bucket"

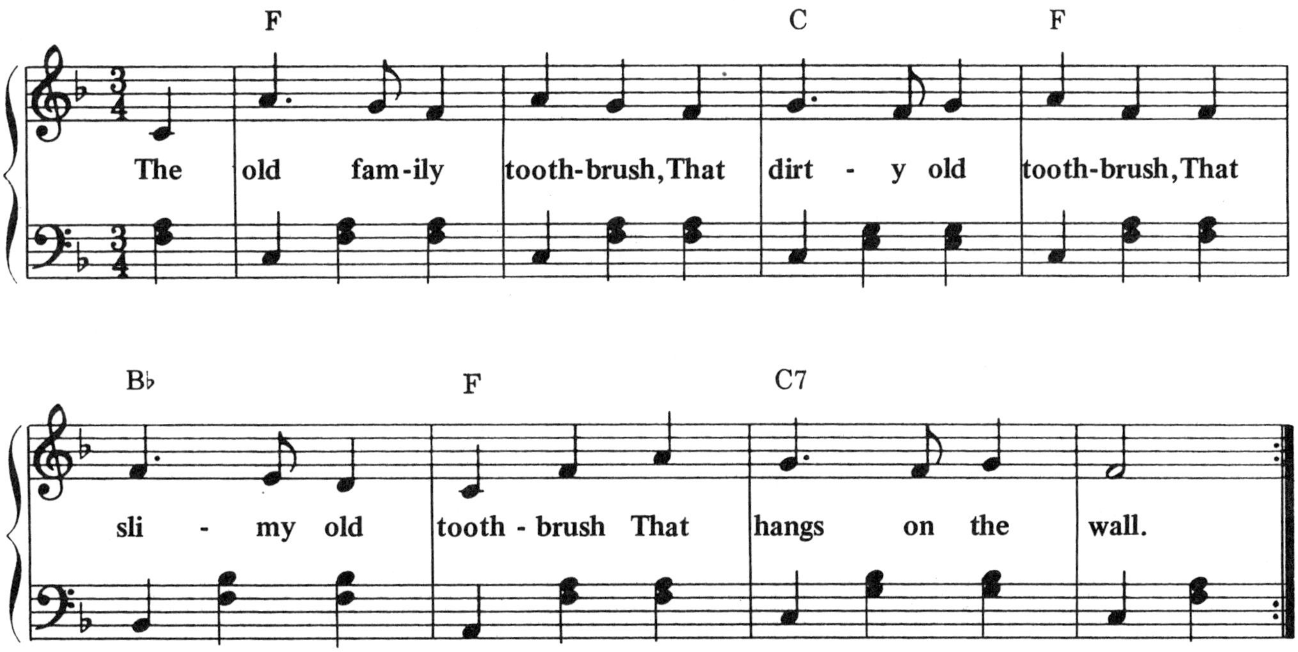

The old family toothbrush,
That dirty old toothbrush,
That slimy old toothbrush
That hangs on the wall.

Oh, first it was Father's,
And then it was Mother's,
And next it was Sister's
And now it is mine.

Oh, Father he used it,
And Mother abused it,
And Sister refused it,
And now it is mine.

The old family toothbrush,
That dirty old toothbrush,
That slimy old toothbrush
That hangs on the wall.

There's a Hole in the Bucket

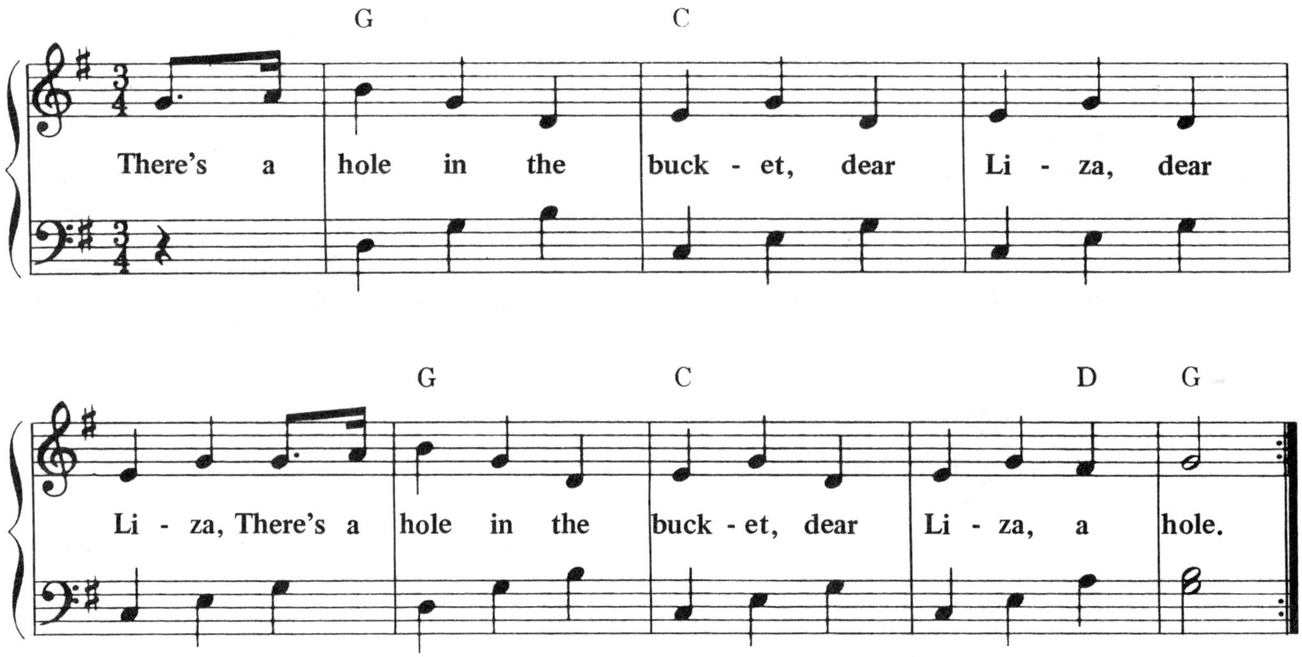

There's a hole in the bucket, dear Liza,
dear Liza,
There's a hole in the bucket, dear Liza,
a hole.

Then mend it, dear Henry, dear Henry,
dear Henry,
Then mend it, dear Henry, dear Henry,
mend it.

With what shall I mend it, dear Liza,
dear Liza,
With what shall I mend it, dear Liza,
with what?

With straw, dear Henry, dear Henry,
dear Henry,
With straw, dear Henry, dear Henry,
with straw.

The straw is too long, dear Liza, dear
Liza,
The straw is too long, dear Liza, too
long.

Then cut it, dear Henry, dear Henry,
dear Henry,
Then cut it, dear Henry, dear Henry,
cut it.

With what shall I cut it, dear Liza, dear
Liza,
With what shall I cut it, dear Liza, with
what?

With a knife, dear Henry, dear Henry,
dear Henry,
With a knife, dear Henry, dear Henry,
a knife.

The knife is too blunt, dear Liza, dear
Liza,
The knife is too blunt, dear Liza, too
blunt.

Then sharpen it, dear Henry, dear
Henry, dear Henry,
Then sharpen it, dear Henry, dear
Henry, sharpen it.

There's a Hole in the Bucket

With what shall I sharpen it, dear Liza,
dear Liza,
With what shall I sharpen it, dear Liza,
with what?

With a stone, dear Henry, dear Henry,
dear Henry,
With a stone, dear Henry, dear Henry,
a stone.

But the stone is too dry, dear Liza,
dear Liza,
But the stone is too dry, dear Liza, too
dry.

Then wet it, dear Henry, dear Henry,
dear Henry,
Then wet it, dear Henry, dear Henry,
wet it.

With what shall I wet it, dear Liza, dear
Liza,
With what shall I wet it, dear Liza, with
what?

With water, dear Henry, dear Henry,
dear Henry,
With water, dear Henry, dear Henry,
with water.

In what shall I get it, dear Liza, dear
Liza,
In what shall I get it, dear Liza, in
what?

In a bucket, dear Henry, dear Henry,
dear Henry,
In a bucket, dear Henry, dear Henry, in
a bucket.

But there's a hole in the bucket, dear
Liza, dear Liza,
There's a hole in the bucket, dear Liza,
a hole.

John Jacob Jingleheimer Schmidt

John Jacob Jingleheimer Schmidt—
His name is my name, too.
Whenever we go out,
The people always shout:
"There goes John Jacob Jingleheimer
Schmidt"—
Dah, dah, dah, dah, dah, dah, dah,"

(*and repeat*).

Rise and Shine

Oh, rise and shine, and give God your
glory, glory,
Rise and shine, and give God your
glory, glory,
Rise and shine, and (*clap*) give God
your glory, glory,
Children of the Lord!

The Lord said to Noah, "There's gonna
be a flood-y, flood-y,"
The Lord said to Noah, "There's gonna
be a flood-y, flood-y.
Get your children (*clap*) out of the
muddy, muddy"
Children of the Lord!

Rise and Shine

The Lord said to Noah, "You'd better
build an ark-y, ark-y,"
Lord said to Noah, "You'd better build
an ark-y, ark-y,
Build it out of (*clap*) birchy bark-y,
bark-y,"
Children of the Lord!

The animals they came in, they came in
by two-sy, two-sy,
Animals, they came in, they came in by
two-sy, two-sy,
Elephants and (*clap*) kangaroo-sy,
roo-sy,
Children of the Lord!

It rained and rained for 40 nights and 40
daysies,
Rained and rained for 40 nights and 40
daysies,
Drove those animals (*clap*) nearly
crazy, crazy,
Children of the Lord!

Noah, he looked up and saw a dove-y,
dove-y,
Noah, he looked up and saw a dove-y,
dove-y,
Saw it up in (*clap*) heaven above-y,
bove-y,
Children of the Lord!

Rise and Shine

The sun came out and dried up the
land-y, land-y
Sun came out and dried up the land-y,
land-y,
Everything was (*clap*) fine and dandy,
dandy,
Children of the Lord!

The animals came off, came off by
threesies, threesies,
Animals came off, came off by three-
sies, threesies,
They'd heard about those (*clap*) birds
and beesies, beesies,
Children of the Lord!

This is the end of, the end of my song,
song,
This is the end of, the end of my song,
song,
Hope it's not too (*clap*) long, long,
long,
Children of the Lord!

This is the end of, the end of my story,
story,
This is the end of, the end of my story,
story,
Everything is (*clap*) hunky dory, dory,
Children of the Lord!

Rise and shine and give God your glory,
glory,
Rise and shine and give God your glory,
glory,
Rise and shine and (*clap*) give God your
glory, glory,
Children of the Lord!

The Slithery D

The slithery D
Slipped into the sea.
It got all the others,
But it won't get me.

Oh, you won't get me,
You slithery D.
You got all the others,
But you won't get . . . .

INDEX OF FIRST LINES

INDEX